Google Adwords

THE ULTIMATE MARKETING GUIDE FOR BEGINNERS TO ADVERTISING ON GOOGLE SEARCH ENGINE WITH PPC USING PROVEN OPTIMIZATION SECRETS

Descrierea CIP a Bibliotecii Naţionale a României

Google Adwords. The Ultimate Marketing Guide for Beginners to Advertising on Google Search Engine with Ppc Using Proven Optimization Secrets. – Bucharest: My Ebook Publishing House, 2018
    ISBN 978-606-983-604-0

Google Adwords

THE ULTIMATE MARKETING GUIDE FOR BEGINNERS
TO ADVERTISING ON GOOGLE SEARCH ENGINE WITH
PPC USING PROVEN OPTIMIZATION SECRETS

My Ebook Publishing House
Bucharest, 2018

CONTENTS

INTRODUCTION

I want to thank you and congratulate you for buying this book, Google Adwords: The Ultimate Marketing Guide For Beginners To Advertising On Google Search Engine With Ppc Using Proven Optimization Secrets.

This book contains proven steps and strategies on how to get your business popular and advertise locally or globally in a more accountable and flexible way, allowing customers and anyone searching on Google for the things you offer to see your business or anything you offer easily by just following few steps provided in this book.

Thanks again for purchasing this book, I hope you enjoy it!

This document is geared towards providing exact and reliable information in regards to the topic and issue covered. The publication is sold with the idea that the publisher is not required to render accounting, officially permitted, or otherwise, qualified services. If advice is necessary, legal or professional, a practiced individual in the profession should be ordered.

- From a Declaration of Principles which was accepted and approved equally by a Committee of the American Bar Association and a Committee of Publishers and Associations.

In no way is it legal to reproduce, duplicate, or transmit any part of this document in either electronic means or in printed format. Recording of this publication is strictly prohibited and any storage of this document is not allowed unless with written permission from the publisher. All rights reserved.

The information provided herein is stated to be truthful and consistent, in that any liability, in terms of inattention or otherwise, by any usage or abuse of any policies, processes, or directions contained within is the solitary and utter responsibility of the recipient reader. Under no circumstances will any legal responsibility or blame be held against the publisher for any reparation, damages, or monetary loss due to the information herein, either directly or indirectly.

Respective authors own all copyrights not held by the publisher.

The information herein is offered for informational purposes solely, and is universal as so. The presentation of the information is without contract or any type of guarantee assurance.

The trademarks that are used are without any consent, and the publication of the trademark is without permission or backing by the trademark owner. All trademarks and brands within this book are for clarifying purposes only and are the owned by the owners themselves, not affiliated with this document.

Chapter 1
Google Adwords

Google Adwords is Google's advertising system that displays or advertise your business or anything you offer on Google's search results. Advertisers bid on certain keywords for their clickable ads to appear in Google Search results.

This advertisement system by Google helps you attract more customers without personally meeting them. Google Adwords also help to bring in new website visitors and reach your business out to the world.

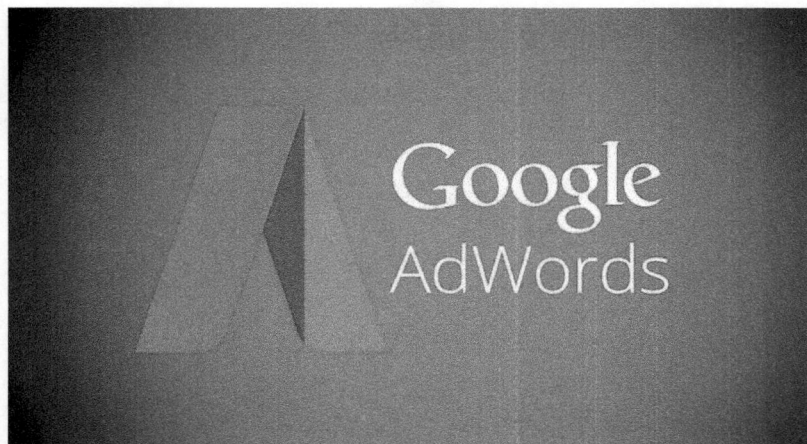

Source: Neilpatel.com

Google Adwords works simply and understandably whereby your business gets found and seen by people on Google when they search for things you offer. That is, I sign up to Google Adwords and register, follow simple steps that are going to be explained in the next chapter and, my business is out there when you search for it using related keywords.

Targeting your advertisements to customers in individual countries or cities in a more accountable and flexible way, also knowing how far and well your advertisements is helping your business grow.

Google Adwords sends monthly summary listings of all key stats and numbers that matter and gets your business across the globe.

Signing up for Google Adwords is free, and you can tweak your ads, try new search words or items, start, stop, pause or test your advertisement too. Here, business owners pay per click that is when a customer clicks on your ad is when you pay, you have no contact to lock you in, allowing you to stop or pause at any time.

Advertisers pay only for results and work on flexible budgeting that allows you to set how much you want to pay each time someone clicks on your ad and change it at any time. Payment options are made easy, either using a regular credit or debit card(Visa, MasterCard or visa electron) and also via bank payment methods.

Being just a Google Search away from your customers is not something to miss out. Search ads are built within just a few minutes with just the very right guide which I hope to provide to you dear reader. Simply done by writing an ad that tells people what you offer.

Choosing keywords that potential customers might search for on Google for the things you offer comes next in mind, this is to locate customers to your adverts easily. Budgeting is also crucial since Google AdWords works such that you only pay per click then you choose an amount suitably okay for you.

Chapter 2

Guide To Using Google Adwords

In this chapter, a comprehensive and well-explained method/guide will be given on how to use and work with Google Adwords. First starting off with things to know about Google Adwords and then steps to follow to make your business grow and large using Google Adwords.

Adword Basis.

First, you must be using a supported browser such as Google Chrome, Firefox, Safari or internet explorer or have them installed on your desktop computer. For Android devices, the Adword Android App is recommended which can be downloaded from Google Play Store.

Before creating an Adword account, you must think up a very catchy advert. Advertising on Google Adwords requires you to have a website that's because Google Adwords will link up your online ad to your website. If you don't have a website, one can be created for free or a local page with Google My Business and advertise with ad express.

After creating a website and signing up on Google Adwords, you're currency and time zone will also be needed. Your time zone can be changed, but your currency remains the same, so these settings must be done carefully because they are used to determine how you will be billed and also how your account will run.

Users can register and fix their payment currencies in dollars or in the currency of their country of residence. This is because certain currencies can be used in only some countries so choose carefully. Choosing to pay with another currency requires you to create a new Adword account.

Your report and statistics are affected by the time zone chosen by you; an Adword amount can be set for most of the standard time zones in the world.

Note: Your time zone selection doesn't affect the location where your ad may show.

Campaign Settings:

Advertising with Google Adwords starts with creating a good campaign.

Campaign settings are also required, so you have to choose the right campaign settings to help your ads. It is also possible for you to adjust your campaign settings to help you tailor your campaign. A campaign name is required although Adword enters a default campaign name for you. A name that describes the theme of your campaign should be registered to get to customers easily. Note that your campaign name is not visible to your customers.

Campaign types are based on advertising goals so choose one based on your goals. Example, if I want my Ad to be shown on Google.com, I will select a 'search network' campaign to get more visitors.

Network Settings:

Network settings indicate where your ads will appear based on the type of campaign chosen. For example, your ads can be shown on Google Search networks and also on non-Google Search sites that partner with Google to display advertisements. Your campaign ads show to customers that set their browser language to your targeted language and also to customers within the targeted geographic locations.

Billing and Budgets:

Bidding and budget can be manually set for clicks on your ads or probably let Adword do it for you. Additional bidding options may be seen depending on your type of campaign. Also, note that your budget should be the average amount you are comfortable with spending on your campaign each day and can be adjusted anytime to suit you.

Importantly, for your ads, more information such as location, tips and what your business is about, page links and phone number should be added using the ad extension.

Some additional options are also present to help you optimize your campaign. These features are optional. You can schedule a campaign start and end date. Choosing specific days or time of the week you want your ad to show is also made available for you.

To get your Ads running, your billing information has to be submitted. First sign in to your account, click the gear icon and choose billing and payments. Select your country where your billing address is located from the drop-down menu, billing options available for your country and location will be seen. Make selections and follow steps provided to enter your billing information.

Add a backup credit card if you are on an alternative payment which means you only pay after your ad has been clicked or started running. A back-up credit card is highly recommended in case your primary payment method doesn't work. This is to keep your ad running.

Showing Results:

On personal computers on smartphones, if your keywords match the words people search for Google, your ad can appear above the search results provided by Google. You should make sure your customers notice the type of brand, consider your offerings and want to click on your ads, use eye-catching words and descriptions. Creating different adverts to see which performs best can also be an option for you.

Reach Out To the World In Every Way

Over 2 million websites and 650000 apps can show ads to wherever your audience or customers are.

Ways to Display Adverts

Source: auxanographicdesigns.com

- Texts: Url's, lines of text that are catchy and headlines help advertise on a Google search.

- Gmails: You can also show your custom ads in Gmail so that people can expand your ads in their inbox, they can also save and forward your ads to other customers and friends.
- Banner: Images or media shouldn't skip your mind, adverts let you include customized layouts, elements, interactives, animations and more.
- Apps: Ads can also show on apps, you can create a campaign targeting specific kinds of Mobile App categories.

Display Ads Explanation

Whether using images or making text ads with the ad gallery included in your AdWords account, only a few minutes can fetch you, a great number of customers.

Deciding Where Your Ads Will Run

Display ads permit the creation of highly targeted campaigns based on what you offer and know about your customers such as interests and demographics.

With millions of websites, news pages, blogs, Gmails, YouTube and all, specialized options for targeting keywords, demographics, re-marketing, etc. Is also made available. You can encourage your customers to see your breaks and consider working with you, also making them put it into action.

Targeting specific audience interests like music lovers, news lovers, outdoor and nightlife enthusiasts, pet and animal lovers, video lovers, technophiles, etc. Can also help trigger ad performance.

Always Improve

Always improve, fine-tune and tweak your ads, you can never tell which will do better. Firstly, measuring your ads results and then figure out which most audiences are receptive to. Whether you are looking to get more texts, calls, or to increase sales, Adwords help you measure campaign performance and allow you to make adjustments to meet your objectives.

Video Ads

Don't bother about showing your ads to people who are not interested in what you offer, video ads only show to people you want to see your ad, and you only pay when they watch.

Preview of Video Ads

Getting your ad live should be one of your tactics for getting more customers and business growth. Once you create a video, set up a YouTube account and upload it. Then Adwords can be used to start your campaign on YouTube. Note that your video will appear before or next to related videos in search results. Remember always to choose where your video ad will appear. Whether you are referring to music lovers, sports fans, politics lovers, males, females or anyone else, you can also choose your audience based on age, gender, interest, location and more.

You will not want to advertise to people who do not want to see your ads. Also, decide how much you want to spend on your ad when watched. You can use Google Analytics tool to see what's working.

YouTube reaches more 18-49 year olds by research than any cable network. With over one billion users on YouTube, you can select the audience you want. During the preview of your ads on YouTube, you only pay when your ad is being watched. If skipped before 30 second or the end, you don't pay.

See and Know What's Working

Use YouTube's Analytics Tool to understand who is watching your ads and how they are interacting with them. Since you have complete control of your budget, you can spend what you are comfortable with.

App Ads

Google Adwords is not restricted to app advertisement. You can also reach users who will love and want to download your app. Universal App Campaigns help you promote your app whether iOS or Android, billions of users will be able to see it on Google all from one campaign. Let Google machine learning help you find the best users and help you make the most out of your budget. This means that you don't have to bother about the type of audience you set to view your ad. Let Google do the work.

Setting Up

Find and customize your Android or IOS app to see a custom ad preview using information from the App Store or Play Store.

Then you text, upload images and videos of your app. This will do well to help attract your app lovers. Decide how much you are willing to spend for each install of your app (Cost per Install).

Launch your ad and allow Google to do the hard work. Google will automatically show your ad across Google Search, play, YouTube and more. Your ads, bids, and targeting are continually refined to deliver high quality installs within your set budget or CPI.

Expand Within or Globally

You can reach out to potential customers within or globally; it is up to you to decide on how you want to advertise your business.

How to Make the Best Out of Google Adwords

These days, customers take decisions faster, so it's crucial to engage customers with targeted messages and keywords at the moment that matters. Create more than one ad per group and always optimize how they show. The one most relevant to the query gets selected.

Google shows the ad predicted to have the highest chance of getting you the clicks and customers you want. Add multiple extensions by using ad extensions. This enables your ad to get more visits. It also gives your customers more information about what you offer, be it your business, products or services even before they click. Ad extension boosts ad performance.

Improve your quality, budget, and bids to be more competitive in the ad auction and get more impressions.

Chapter 3
Writing Successful Text Ads

To effectively reach out to customers worldwide, your text ads should include relevant, attractive, empowering and specific topics

- Highlight what makes you unique to your customers, things like free shipping, discount available, etc. Tell people what to benefit from you and also showcase the product, services and offers that make you competitive. Include prices, promotions, exclusives.

Give to your potential customers what they need to decide because people also search on Google for decisions and what to do. Also, state if you have a limited discount or stock of any exclusive product.

• Empower customers to take action.

Calls to action like purchase now, call today, browse, sign up, etc. Make clear what steps to take if you are selling something or offering a service. Also, include at least one of your keywords for example if you added *plumbing* as a keyword, your ad headline could be *'get affordable plumbing services.'*

• Match your ad to your landing page

Check out the page that you are linking to from your ad (this page referred to as the landing page). Also, make sure that the promotion or product of your ad is included on your website.

• Let your customers find you easily

People are more likely to know or like to call you when they see your ad. Show your location and phone number with location extensions and call extensions.

• Check for common add text mistakes.

Check for strange capitalizations, wrong or incomplete URLs, phone numbers and more in order to make sure all AdWords are of high quality and to meet high performance with editorial standards.

Bidding Strategies

Good Adwords users place their ads in auctions which are run by Google to find the ads that show when someone searches on

Google. A bidding strategy is needed to place your ads in an auction and get it viewed on Google Search.

Cost per click: in this strategy, you focus on getting clicks on your ads, methods suitable for those who want to build traffic on their website.

Cost per impression: in this strategy, you focus your mind on the number of times your ad shows for those who want to build on their brand name and image.

Cost per acquisition: a strategy related to the conversion rate of customers. This is suitable to promote purchases for already established advertisers.

Quality Score

This is the relevance and quality of your ad in which Google measures to see if your ad is useful to customers and if they click on the ad, they will need to be taken to the desired page. The higher the quality score, the better. This improves the rate at which your ad is shown even if your ad has a low bid. Quality score is dependent on factors like account performance, ad relevance, click through rate(CTR).

Checking quality score

Each keyword gets a score between one to ten which is from the lowest to the highest. There are several ways to check your ad quality score. The easiest way is to look in the keywords tab.

Keywords diagnosis can be run by;

1. First click on the campaign tab

2. Then select the keywords tab

3. Near the keywords status, there is a white speech bubble. Clicking on this bubble will show you details of your quality score.

4. You Will also be able to check on the landing page experience of visitors, relevance of ad and click through rate.

You can also check the quality score by enabling the quality score column.

Ad Rank

This is known as the ranking given to an ad based on its bid and quality score. All ads are primarily placed in an order that is placed on the ad rank. When you search for an ad on Google, the ad with the most ad appears in the top position and is seen first. You can determine your ad rank by multiplying your quality score and your bid.

An amount known as the discounter is the minimum amount an advertiser is to pay to display an ad and defeat the ad rank of the rival ad placed above them. Knowing your ad rank is important also provided here are components that can help improve your ad rank.

Your landing page: the quality of your landing page must be of high standards containing rich information easy to navigate and more. This is to improve your ad rank by improving your ad quality score.

Click through rate: your click-through rate is also an important factor. This can be improved by improving impressions of your ad, historical clicks, extensions, the position of your ad and other such factors.

Ad relevance: Texts and information given by the ad must be relevant to what customers search for performance on targeted devices is also key. Your ad must be able to work well on all devices it targets including computers, mobile phones, tablets, etc.

Geographic Factors: the geographic location that you have chosen as the targeted audience should be significantly affected by your campaign audience.

When Your Advertisement Start Running

For certain payment methods, your ads start running as soon as your billing information has been submitted. Other payment methods may cause ads to start running after a week or less due to payment verification and processing time.

Get Your First Advertisement

After creating ads, it is important to ensure that they are working and appearing to customers. The ad preview and diagnosis tool can be used to check your account, see statistics and know whether your advertisements are working.

It is recommended to use the ad preview and diagnosis tool instead of searching for your ad on Google.com. Also if you repeatedly look for your ad without clicking it, it might not be shown by Google again, this is because Google system will assume you are not interested in it again.

If you cannot determine why your ads are not displaying from your ad preview and diagnosis tool, the following list of possible options can be checked out;

Check that your ads are enabled and approved. This is done by clicking ads and extensions in the left page menu. An enabled ad will show a green dot next to its name. To enable a paused ad, click the pause icon and then click enable.

Also, check that your ads are getting traffic from customers. You can also check that your keywords are triggering ads. Also, check your targeted customers and review your target location. Importantly, reviewing the Google advertisement policy is a key step to getting your ads up and running.

Tracking your goals will help you advertise your business more, checking statistics and keywords, what your ads talk about also increases output. Review of performance determines whether to tweak and fine-tune your account by either changing your keywords or increasing your payment to allow Google to always show your ads. Checking monthly summary listings and statistics sent to you from Adword helps to know how your ads are doing and promoting your business.

Finding new customers is also increased by making the most of display advertising. Check that you are accurately tracking website and app conversations, this is because your ability to optimize your Ad is only as good as the data you are using. Also, keep search and display campaigns separate for more control because search and display ads reach customers in different contexts.

Re-engage past site visitors with remarking by either removing exclusions for languages, location, and placement, using dynamic re-marketing to show the most personalized ad possible.

Responsive and image ads in multiple sizes can be used. Exclude low performing site categories and placements by avoiding contents your target audience are less likely to visit. Expand your target locations also so as to reach more people and also drive sales with Gmail ads.

Adjusting bids by either increasing pay per click can be made to maximize profit, this way Google show your ads more often.

Optimize your Website and Adword ads for Mobile Devices

Investing your money in making your website and AdWords ads mobile friendly is important. This shows up higher in search results; major traffic comes from people on their mobile phones.

Expand your text ads also for optimal performances on mobile devices by uploading your existing texts ads to the expanded text ads. Note that there is no cost to do so.

46

Using the right ad extension for mobile will allow you to show extra business info with your ads like address, phone number, page links, etc. Always preview your ads to be sure that they perform well on devices such that they are neither too small or big.

Chapter 4
Google Adwords and How to Use Them

With the information provided, you are less likely to face a problem using Google Adwords. I present to you a synopsis of my book: Google Adwords.

1. Choose your keywords wisely

One benefit of using Google Adwords is that you can target your ads to people interested in the products you offer. There are the right keywords which ought to be used in order to that generate traffic and brings in more customers. A tool known as Google keywords planner can also be used to find new and beneficial keywords relating to your product along with search volume data and trends to give you an idea of some impressions and clicks you are likely to make. Collect enough keywords, analyze them and form it into excellent keywords.

2. Be as real/straightforward as possible

The last thing you will want is to pay for clicks that don't matter. If people are clicking on your ad and do not find what they need on your website, it is a waste of the money you paid for that Adword click. If you sell used products or scrap materials, make it clear that what you sell is used products and not just products or scrap materials and not just materials. This enhances your campaign and makes good use of your product.

3. Create targeted Ad/copies

Creating copies of your keywords to target your customers is recommended. You can edit and change your keywords as time goes on to which one gets more clicks and brings more customers.

4. Be unique

It's not bad to take a look at what your competitors offer, see what they do not offer too and bring it in your ad. Offers like discount available, free shipping, warranty and so on, can also be added to deals and promotions to make you stand out from the rest. Call to action like free downloads to draw customers and learn more to encourage them.

5. Lead to a Suitable Landing Page

Remember a homepage is not a landing page unless it has been tailored to meet needs of a perfect landing page which gives customers across to information they need. It is recommended to make each product you offer have their own page so as to increase traffic in your website and also make it easy for your customers to navigate. Your landing page should start off from where your ad ends. Always remember to add call to action buttons like subscribe here, sign up, download, call and so on.

6. Match keywords on your Landing Page

To make your landing page better, it is important to add your keywords to your landing page too. Including searched words will increase your Google quality score and also reduce the cost of your ads. A few good keywords will do.

7. Aim for a higher quality score

Google provides a quality score for all PPC campaigns determined by the following factors; CTR, ad relevance, historical Adword performance. Click through rate is the most important of all. your overall score will help determine your position on Google Search page. A higher quality score results in a low cost per conversion. It shows that your ad is relevant do Google will charge you less for clicks. steps to achieve a high quality score includes;

- Optimise landing page
- Refine ad text
- Conduct keyword research
- Organize keywords
- Be real.

8. Use Ad Extensions

This is a way of including extra information for potential customers and making your ad mostly sought for on the search results page. Not all adds are eligible to show extensions. Actually, ads with extensions carry a higher cost per click due to competition over using them.

9. Create precise Ad Groups

You can always optimize your campaigns to determine ad success. create similarly themed campaigns and ad groups. You should keep all your related keywords in one add group and monitor the cost and effectiveness of all your keywords.

10. Use Location Targeting

To reduce cost from unwanted visitors clicking your ad, it is important to target your ads to a specific location for broad match terms. For example, if you are targeting people searching for plumbing services in your area, they will need to search for plumbing services and find you if they are in your targeted area. You can then set a separate national campaign with no location limitation, this way your ad is one restricted to a particular region.

11. Scheduling your ads to work at specific times

This is done to reduce cost. You can set your ads to run, show at specific times, probably those times you are going to be available to your customers. This can be done on the Ad schedule sub tab.

12. Conduct a Test

You can create two ads with different elements which include the headline, first line, second line and display URL. A more obvious result is gotten from the test. You can also change few items in the different ads and run a test on which ad performs best.

13. Optimize your Ads for both web and mobile

Google now gives the opportunity to adjust bids for different devices. For example, if you want to focus more on mobile device experience, you can raise your bid on mobile devices so that more of your budget will cover this area. This is to allocate your budget effectively and also increase the number of relevant clicks.

14. Regularly Check your Budget

Always view the data for your campaign regularly. You should also assess your budget and see where they are working well.

I mean that you should also check to know your budget so as to either increase or lower your bid. This is done to always keep your ads running.

15. Monitor your Campaign Frequently

It is easier to think that once you have set up a campaign you feel is fully you can just let it run at its own course. This might not bring in more conversions and make you profit. Monitoring your campaigns regularly helps you to know the success of your campaign, knowing when market competition changes and knowing when to adjust bids to continue ranking high. This is done to get the most out of PPC campaign and make high profit.

If you don't have much time to monitor your campaigns, you can always find someone to do it for you. This helps you to not spend much on less because as your ad runs on Google you spend money on clicks. You could also get a PPC agent to help you which will cost you but also ensure that your campaign is being monitored.

Why spend time moving around from person to person telling them what you offer and your business when you can also spend some time on Google Adword campaigns and reach out to more people around the world. A fast, reliable, flexible, accountable and ready way to advertise.

Conclusion

Thank you again for purchasing this book!

I hope this book was able to help you know more about Google Adwords and guide you towards making the best out of your business by advertising to the world in a more accountable, easy and flexible and fast way.

The next step is to follow these steps provided, Just create an account, think up a very good campaign, target your location, set your budget, write your first ad and decide where you would like it to appear. I will love to see your business when I search on Google.

Finally, if you enjoyed this book, then I'd like to ask you for a favor, would you be kind enough to leave a review for this book? It'd be greatly appreciated!

Thank you and good luck!